AD&D 2nd Edition Thief Screen

Accessory

AF683154

Rogue Prerequisites

	Ability Scores	Alignment	Race	Multiclassed?
Bard	Dex 12+, Int 13+ Cha 15+	Any neutral	H, Half-elf	No
Thief	Dex 9+	Any except LG	Any	Yes

Prime Requisites: Thieves with a Dexterity of 16 or greater earn 10% additional experience Bards with a Dexterity and Charisma of 16 or greater earn 10% additional experience.

Thieving Skill Base Scores

Class	Pick Pockets	Open Locks	Find/ Remove Traps	Move Silently	Hide in Shadows	Detect Noise	Climb Walls	Read Languages
Thief[1]	15%	10%	5%	10%	5%	15%	60%	0%
Bard[2]	10%	—	—	—	—	20%	50%	5%

1. Plus 60 discretionary points at 1st level (maximum of 30 can be applied to any single skill) and 30 discretionary points at each level thereafter (maximum of 15 can be applied to any single skill).
2. Plus 20 discretionary points at 1st level (to be assigned as the player wishes) and 15 discretionary points at each level thereafter (to be assigned as the player wishes).

Thieving Skill Racial Adjustments

Skill	Dwarf	Elf	Gnome	Half-elf	Halfling
Pick Pockets	—	+5%	—	+10%	+5%
Open Locks	+10%	–5%	+5%	—	+5%
Find/Remove Traps	+15%	—	+10%	—	+5%
Move Silently	—	+5%	+5%	—	+10%
Hide in Shadows	—	+10%	+5%	+5%	+15%
Detect Noise	—	+5%	+10%	—	+5%
Climb Walls	–10%	—	–15%	—	–15%
Read Languages	–5%	—	—	—	–5%

Thieving Skill Dexterity Adjustments

Dexterity	Pick Pockets	Open Locks	Find/ Remove Traps	Move Silently	Hide in Shadows
9	–15%	–10%	–10%	–20%	–10%
10	–10%	–5%	10%	–15%	–5%
11	–5%	—	–5%	–10%	—
12	—	—	—	–5%	—
13-15	—	—	—	—	—
16	—	+5%	—	—	—
17	+5%	+10%	—	+5%	+5%
18	+10%	+15%	+5%	+10%	+10%
19	+15%	+20%	+10%	+15%	+15%
20	+20%	+25%	+12%	+20%	+17%
21	+25%	+27%	+15%	+25%	+20%
22	+27%	+30%	+17%	+30%	+22%

Thieving Skill Armor Adjustments

Skill	No Armor[1]	Elven Chain	Studded or Padded	Hide	Ring or Chain	Brigandine or Splint	Scale or Banded	Plate Mail[2]	Plate Armor[3]
Pick Pockets	+5%	–20%	–30%	–60%	–40%	–40%	–50%	–75%	–95%
Open Locks	—	–5%	–10%	–50%	–15%	–15%	–20%	–40%	–80%
Find/Remove Traps	—	–5%	–10%	–50%	–15%	–25%	–20%	–40%	–80%
Move Silently	+10%	–10%	–20%	–30%	–40%	–40%	–60%	–80%	–95%
Hide in Shadows[4]	+5%	–10%	–20%	–20%	–30%	–30%	–50%	–75%	–95%
Detect Noise	—	–5%	–10%	–10%	–20%	–25%	–30%	–50%	–70%
Climb Walls	+10%	–20%	–30%	–60%	–40%	–50%	–90%	–95%	–95%
Read Languages	—	—	—	—	—	—	—	—	—

1. This category applies when wearing protective devices such as rings, cloaks, and bracers.
2. Includes bronze plate mail.
3. Includes both field plate and full plate armor.
4. Assumes the armor is covered by another garment. Elven chain mail is light and thin, and can be worn under normal clothing. All other types of armor except leather are stiff or bulky and can be covered only by a full body cloak.

Rogue Experience Levels

Level	Thief/ Bard	Hit Dice (d6)
1	0	1
2	1,250	2
3	2,500	3
4	5,000	4
5	10,000	5
6	20,000	6
7	40,000	7
8	70,000	8
9	110,000	9
10	160,000	10
11	220,000	10+2
12	440,000	10+4
13	660,000	10+6
14	880,000	10+8
15	1,100,000	10+10
16	1,320,000	10+12
17	1,540,000	10+14
18	1,760,000	10+16
19	1,980,000	10+10
20	2,200,000	10+20

Bard Spell Progression

Bard Level	Spell Level 1	2	3	4	5	6
1	—	—	—	—	—	—
2	1	—	—	—	—	—
3	2	—	—	—	—	—
4	2	1	—	—	—	—
5	3	1	—	—	—	—
6	3	2	—	—	—	—
7	3	2	1	—	—	—
8	3	3	1	—	—	—
9	3	3	2	—	—	—
10	3	3	2	1	—	—
11	3	3	3	1	—	—
12	3	3	3	2	—	—
13	3	3	3	2	1	—
14	3	3	3	3	1	—
15	3	3	3	3	2	—
16	4	3	3	3	2	1
17	4	4	3	3	3	1
18	4	4	4	3	3	2
19	4	4	4	4	3	2
20	4	4	4	4	4	3

Rogue Proficiency Slots

Weapon Proficiencies

Initial	#Levels	Penalty
2	4	–3

Nonweapon Proficiencies

Initial	#Levels
3	4

Extra Nonweapon Proficiencies (Optional Rule)

Intelligence 2–8: 1; *9–11:* 2; *12–13:* 3; *14–15:* 4; *16:* 5; *17:* 6; *18:* 7; *19:* 8; *20:* 9; *21:* 10; *22:* 11; *23:* 12; *24:* 15; *25:* 20.

Thief Weapons Chart

Item	Cost	Weight (lbs)	Size	Type†	Speed Factor	—Damage— S–M	L
Bow	—	—	—	—	—	—	—
Composite short bow	75 gp	2	M	—	6	—	—
Flight arrow	12/3 sp	‡	M	P	—	1d6	1d6
Long bow	75 gp	3	L	—	8	—	—
Sheaf arrow	6/3 cp	‡	M	P	—	1d8	1d8
Stone arrow, flight	12/3 cp	1/10	M	P	—	1d4	1d4
Short bow	30 gp	2	M	—	7	—	—
Club	—	3	M	B	4	1d6	1d3
Crossbow	—	—	—	—	—	—	—
Hand quarrel	1 gp	‡	S	P	—	1d3	1d2
Hand crossbow	300 gp	3	S	—	5	—	—
Dagger or dirk	2 gp	1	S	P	2	1d4	1d3
Bone dagger	1 sp	1	S	P	2	1d2	1d2
Parrying dagger	5 gp	1	S	P	2	1d3	1d3
Stone dagger	2 sp	1	S	P	2	1d3	1d2
Dart	5 sp	½	S	P	2	1d3	1d2
Knife	5 sp	½	S	P/S	2	1d3	1d2
Bone knife	3 cp	½	S	P/S	2	1d2	1d2
Stone knife	5 cp	½	S	P/S	2	1d2	1d2
Lasso	5 sp	3	L	—	10	—	—
Quarterstaff	—	4	L	B	4	1d6	1d6
Sling	5 cp	‡	S	—	6	—	—
Sling bullet	1 cp	½	S	B	—	1d4+1	1d6+1
Sling stone	—	½	S	B	—	1d4	1d4
Sword	—	—	—	—	—	—	—
Broad sword	10 gp	4	M	S	5	2d4	1d6+1
Long sword	15 gp	4	M	S	5	1d8	1d12
Short sword	10 gp	3	M	P	3	1d6	1d8

† The "Type" category is divided into bludgeoning (B), piercing (P), and slashing (S).
‡ These items weigh little individually. Ten of these weigh one pound.

Missile Weapon Ranges

Weapon	ROF	Range S	M	L
Comp. short bow	2/1	5	10	18
Short bow	2/1	5	10	15
Club	1	1	2	3
Hand crossbow	1	2	4	6
Dagger	2/1	1	2	3
Dart	3/1	1	2	4
Knife	2/1	1	2	3
Sling bullet	1	5	10	20
Sling stone	1	4	8	16

"ROF" is the rate of fire—how many shots the weapon can fire off in one round. This is independent of the number of melee attacks a character can make in a round. Range is given in *tens of yards*. Each range category (short, medium, or long) includes attacks from distances equal to or less than the given range. Thus a sling bullet flung at a target 80 yards away uses the medium-range modifier.

The modifiers for range are –2 for medium range and –5 for long range.

Backstab Damage Multipliers

Thief's Level	Damage Multiplier
1-4	×2
5-8	×3
9-12	×4
13+	×5

Thieving Skill Thief-Kit Adjustments

Kit	Pick Pockets[1]	Open Locks	Find/ Remove Traps[2]	Move Silently	Hide in Shadows	Detect Noise	Climb Walls	Read Languages
Acrobat	+5%	–5%	–5%	+5%	—	—	+5%	—
Adventurer	—	—	—	—	—	—	—	—
Assassin	—[3]	—	+5%	—	—	—	—	–5%
Bandit	–5%	—	+10%	—[4]	+5%	—	–5%	–5%
Beggar	+10%	–5%	–5%	—	+5%	—	—	–5%
Bounty Hunter	—[3]	—	+5%	—	—	—	–5%	—
Buccaneer	–5%	—	—	—	—	—	—	+5%
Burglar	–5%	+5%	—	—	—	—	+5%	–5%
Cutpurse	+10%	—	—	—	—	—	–5%	–5%
Fence	—	+5%	+5%	–5%	–5%	—	–5%	+5%
Investigator	–5%	—	—	—	—	+5%	—	—
Smuggler	–5%	–5%	—	+5%	+5%	+5%	–5%	—
Spy	—	—	—	—	—	—	—	—
Swindler	—	–5	—	—	—	—	—	+5%
Thug	—	—	—	—	—	—	—	—
Troubleshooter	–10%	+5%	+5	—	—	—	—	—

1. Includes similar feats of manual dexterity, such as legerdemain and slipping poison (see note 3, below).
2. This ability may also be used in the placement of traps.
3. Assassins and bounty hunters are adept at slipping foreign substances (poison, sedatives, etc.) into drinks. Success in such a feat of manual dexterity is determined by a pick pockets roll, and the assassin or bounty hunter gets a +5% to the roll. This special bonus does not apply, however, to picking pockets or to other tasks covered by this ability.
4. In the wilderness, the bandit gets +5% to this ability.

9463XXX0501

Nonweapon Proficiencies: General Group

Proficiency	# of Slots Required	Relevant Ability	Check Modifier
Agriculture	1	Intelligence	0
Animal Handling	1	Wisdom	–1
Animal Training	1	Wisdom	0
Artistic Ability	1	Wisdom	0
Blacksmithing	1	Strength	0
Brewing	1	Intelligence	0
Carpentry	1	Strength	0
Cobbling	1	Dexterity	0
Cooking	1	Intelligence	0
Dancing	1	Dexterity	0
Direction Sense	1	Wisdom	+1
Etiquette	1	Charisma	0
Fire-building	1	Wisdom	–1
Fishing	1	Wisdom	–1
Heraldry	1	Intelligence	0
Languages, Modern	1	Intelligence	0
Leatherworking	1	Intelligence	0
Mining	2	Wisdom	–3
Pottery	1	Dexterity	–2
Riding, Airborne	2	Wisdom	–2
Riding, Land-based	1	Wisdom	+3
Rope Use	1	Dexterity	0
Seamanship	1	Dexterity	+1
Seamstress/Tailor	1	Dexterity	–1
Singing	1	Charisma	0
Stonemasonry	1	Strength	–2
Swimming	1	Strength	0
Weather Sense	1	Wisdom	–1
Weaving	1	Intelligence	–1

Nonweapon Proficiencies: Rogue Group

Proficiency	# of Slots Required	Relevant Ability	Check Modifier
Ancient History	1	Intelligence	–1
Appraising	1	Intelligence	0
Blind-fighting	2	NA	NA
Disguise	1	Charisma	–1
Forgery	1	Dexterity	–1
Gaming	1	Charisma	0
Gem Cutting	2	Dexterity	–2
Juggling	1	Dexterity	–1
Jumping	1	Strength	0
Local History	1	Charisma	0
Musical Instrument	1	Dexterity	–1
Reading Lips	2	Intelligence	–2
Set Snares	1	Dexterity	–1
Tightrope Walking	1	Dexterity	0
Tumbling	1	Dexterity	0
Ventriloquism	1	Intelligence	–2

Nonweapon Proficiencies: Warrior Group

Proficiency	# of Slots Required	Relevant Ability	Check Modifier
Animal Lore	1	Intelligence	0
Armorer	2	Intelligence	–2
Blind Fighting	2	NA	NA
Bowyer/Fletcher	1	Dexterity	–1
Charioteering	1	Dexterity	+2
Endurance	2	Constitution	0
Gaming	1	Charisma	0
Hunting	1	Wisdom	–1
Mountaineering	1	NA	NA
Navigation	1	Intelligence	–2
Running	1	Constitution	–6
Set Snares	1	Dexterity	–1
Survival	2	Intelligence	0
Tracking	2	Wisdom	–6
Weaponsmithing	3	Intelligence	–3

Nonweapon Proficiencies: Wizard Group

Proficiency	# of Slots Required	Relevant Ability	Check Modifier
Ancient History	1	Intelligence	–1
Astrology	2	Intelligence	0
Engineering	2	Intelligence	–3
Gem Cutting	2	Dexterity	–2
Herbalism	2	Intelligence	–2
Languages, Ancient	1	Intelligence	0
Navigation	1	Intelligence	–2
Reading/Writing	1	Intelligence	+1
Religion	1	Wisdom	0
Spellcraft	1	Intelligence	–2

Armor Class Ratings

Type of Armor	AC Rating
None	10
Shield only	9
Leather or padded armor	8
Leather or padded armor & shield, studded leather, or ring mail	7
Studded leather or ring mail & shield, brigandine, scale mail, hide armor	6
Scale mail or hide & shield, chain mail	5
Chain mail & shield, splint mail, banded mail, bronze plate mail	4
Splint mail, banded mail, or bronze plate mail & shield, plate mail	3
Plate mail & shield, field plate armor	2
Field plate armor & shield, full plate armor	1
Full plate armor & shield	0

Standard Modifiers to Initiative

Specific Situation	Modifier
Hasted	–2
Slowed	+2
On higher ground	–1
Set to receive a charge	–2
Wading or slippery footing	+2
Wading in deep water	+4
Foreign environment	+6
Hindered	+3
Waiting	+1

Cover & Concealment Modifiers

Target is:	Cover	Concealment
25% hidden	–2	–1
50% hidden	–4	–2
75% hidden	–7	–3
90% hidden	–10	–4

Thief & Bard Kit Requirements

These outlined kits are taken from *The Complete Thief's Handbook* and *The Complete Bard's Handbook*, and they are not mandatory. The information here lists initial requirements—benefits, hindrances, and role-playing details are described in the *Handbooks*. Players should check with their DMs before deciding on any kit, and the DM can choose not to allow a kit.

Key. **Name**. **Req** Requirements (above class standards); **Ar** Armor allowed (**Standard** means a kit uses all armor allowed to thieves or bards.; **WPr** Weapon proficiencies allowed (**Standard** means the kit uses all weapons normally allowed to thieves; some kits grant weapons not usually used by thieves; and **Any** allows the use of any weapon); **NPr** Nonweapon proficiencies required (**(B)** shows bonus proficiencies the character gains without filling any "slots"); **Races** Race restrictions (**(M)** indicates that these demihumans can be multiclassed with this kit; **(# level)** after a race indicates an advancement limit for that race).

Thief Kits

Acrobat. Req: Str 12+, Dex 14+; Ar: Standard; WPr: Standard; NPr: None; Races: Any except dwarves, halflings and gnomes do not receive kit's special benefits.

Adventurer. Req: None; Ar: Standard; WPr: Standard; NPr: None; Races: Any.

Assassin. Req: Str 12+, Dex 12+, Int 11+; Ar: Standard; WPr: Any; NPr: Trailing, disguise; Races: Any.

Bandit. Req: Str 10+, Con 10+; Ar: Standard; WPr: Standard plus flail, mace, morning star, and war hammer (initial proficiencies must include knife and a bludgeoning weapon); NPr: Survival (choose appropriate terrain type); Races: Any.

Beggar. Req: None; Ar: Standard; WPr: Choose two from club, dagger, dart, knife, sling, or staff; NPr: Begging, disguise, information gathering, observation; Races: Any.

Bounty Hunter. Req: Str 11+, Int 11+, Wis 11+, Dex 11+, Con 11+; Ar: Standard; WPr: Any; NPr: Tracking; Races: Any.

Buccaneer. Req: Con 10+; Ar: Standard; WPr: Standard (cutlass optional per DM approval); NPr: Navigation, seamanship, swimming; Races: Human, half-elf.

Burglar. Req: Str 10+, Dex 13+; Ar: Standard; WPr: Standard; NPr: Alertness, looting; Races: Any.

Cutpurse. Req: None; Ar: Standard; WPr: Standard; NPr: Observation, trailing; Races: Any.

Fence. Req: Int 12+; Ar: Standard; WPr: Standard; NPr: Appraising, information gathering; Races: Any.

Investigator. Req: None; Ar: Standard; WPr: Standard; NPr: Information gathering, observation; Races: Any.

Scout. Req: None; Ar: Standard; WPr: Standard; NPr: Direction sense, tracking; Races: Any.

Smuggler. Req: None; Ar: Standard; WPr: Standard; NPr: None; Races: Any.

Spy. Req: Int 11+; Ar: Standard; WPr: Standard; NPr: Disguise, information gathering, observation; Races: Any.

Swashbuckler. Req: Str 13+, Dex 13+. Int 13+, Cha 13+; Ar: Standard; WPr: Standard and choose one from stiletto, main-gauche, rapier, and sabre (character receives Warrior THAC0 for the weapon chosen and must spend half of all weapon proficiencies gained learning weapons from the special list until all are learned); NPr: Etiquette, tumbling; Races: Any.

Swindler. Req: Cha 12+; Ar: Standard; WPr: Standard; NPr: Fast-talking; Races: Any.

Thug. Req: Str 12+, Con 12+, Int 12 (max); Ar: Standard; WPr: Standard, can use nonthief weapons at the cost of 1 extra slot (+1 extra weapon slot at 1st level); NPr: Intimidation; Races: Human.

Troubleshooter. Req: None; Ar: Standard; WPr: Standard; NPr: Observation; Races: Any.

Bard Kits

True Bard. Req: None; Ar: Standard; WPr: Standard; NPr: Singing (B), musical instrument (B), reading/writing (native tongue) (B), local history (B); Races: Human, half-elf (M).

Blade. Req: Dex 13+; Ar: Standard; WPr: Half of all slots must be spent on the following: sword (any), dagger, knife. The character is limited to only one pure missile weapon (bows or other nonmelee weapons); NPr: Reading/writing (native tongue) (B), local history (B), blind-fighting (B); Races: Human, half-elf (M).

Charlatan. Req: None; Ar: Any appropriate for the character's current role; WPr: Must spend at least one initial slot on dagger, long sword or short sword. Every other slot gained must be spent on these weapons until all are learned; NPr: Acting (B), disguise (B), forgery (B), gaming (B); Races: Human, half-elf, gnome (6th level).

Gallant. Req: None; Ar: Any (elven chain mail preferred); WPr: Initial weapons must include jousting lance; NPr: Dancing (B), etiquette (B), ancient language (B), poetry (B); Races: Human, half-elf.

Gypsy-Bard. Req: None; Ar: Leather, padded, studded leather, hide, or elven chain mail; WPr: Initial weapons must include a dagger or knife (character's first sword, if any, must be a khopesh or scimitar), and the character cannot take use battle axes, lances (any), polearms (any), tridents, two-handed swords, bastard swords, or war hammers; NPr: Dancing (B), direction sense (B), modern language (Gypsy), musical instrument (tambourine, violin or mandolin); Races: Human, half-elf (M), elf (9th level) (M).

Herald. Req: None; Ar: Standard; WPr: Any; NPr: Etiquette (B), heraldry (B), local history, reading/writing (B); Races: Any (all demihumans limited to 6th level).

Jester. Req: Dex 14+; Ar: Leather, padded, studded leather, or elven chain mail; WPr: Blowgun, hand crossbow, dagger, dart, hand axe, javelin, knife, quarter staff, scourge, sling, short sword, and whip; NPr: Acting (B), dancing (B), juggling (B), tumbling (B); Races: Human, half-elf, gnome (15th level), halfling (8th level).

Jongleur. Req: Dex 14+; Ar: Leather, studded leather, padded, or even chain mail; WPr: Hurled weapons (any weapon that can be thrown in combat) plus polearm (any), quarterstaff, sling, staff sling, and whip; NPr: Juggling (B), jumping (B), tightrope walking (B), tumbling (B); Races: Human, half-elf (M), gnome (9th level) (M), halfling (12th level).

Loremaster. Req: Int 14+, Wis 14+; Ar: Leather; WPr: Blowgun, dagger, dart, hand crossbow, knife, quarterstaff, sling, and staff sling; NPr: Ancient history (B), ancient language (B), navigation (B), reading/writing (B); Races: Human, half-elf (M), elf (12th level).

Meistersinger. Req: None; Ar: Standard; WPr: Cannot use harpoon, lance (any), mancatcher, polearm (any), or trident (Initial weapons must include one melee and one missile weapon; the character must thereafter choose weapons in the following repetitive sequence: hurled, melee, missile.); NPr: Animal lore (B), musical instrument (B), singing (B), survival (B); Races: Human, half-elf (M), elf (15th level).

Riddlemaster. Req: Int 15+; Ar: Standard; WPr: Blowgun, bow (any), crossbow (any), dagger, dart, hand axe, javelin, knife, quarterstaff, sling, spear, staff sling, short sword, and whip; NPr: Artistic ability (riddles) (B), modern language (B), poetry (B), reading/writing (B); Races: Human, half-elf (M), gnome (8th level), halfling (9th level).

Skald. Req: None; Ar: Up to bronze plate mail and shield; WPr: Initial weapons must include one of the following: broad sword, hand axe, battle axe, or spear (At least half of all additional slots must be spent on these weapons until all are selected.); NPr: Ancient history (B), local history (B), poetry (B), singing (B); Races: Human, half-elf (M), dwarf (12th level) (M).

Thespian. Req: None; Ar: Any (+1 AC when using armor not allowed to regular bards; the thespian can carry a shield, but gains no benefit from it.); WPr: Limited to three weapon proficiencies: dagger (1st level), knife (2nd level), and short sword (3rd level), with a weapon nonproficiency penalty of –2; NPr: Acting (B), disguise (B), modern language (B), reading/writing (B); Races: Human, half-elf (M).

Dwarven Chanter. Req: Con 13+, Int any; Ar: Any except plate mail or plate armor; WPr: Club, flail (any), mace (any), javelin, morning star, quarterstaff, sling, spear, staff sling, and war hammer; NPr: Chanting (B), crowd working (B), musical instrument (B), spellcraft (B); Races: Dwarf (15th level) (M).

Elven Minstrel. Req: None; Ar: Leather, padded, or elven chain mail; WPr: Blowgun, bow (any), dagger, dart, hand axe, javelin, knife, quarterstaff, sling, spear, staff sling, long sword, short sword, and trident; NPr: Musical instrument (B), reading/writing (B), singing (B), spellcraft (B); Races: Elf (15th level) (M), half-elf (12th level) (M).

Gnome Professor. Req: Int 15+, Cha 13+; Ar: Leather, studded leather, or padded. The character can experiment with other armor types for 1d10 days each month (this causes a +1 armor class penalty and negates dexterity bonuses to armor class); WPr: Arquebus, blowgun, bow (any), crossbow (any), harpoon, mancatcher, scourge, sling, staff sling, and whip; NPr: Ancient history (B), ancient language (B), modern language (B), reading/writing (B); Races: Gnome (15th level) (M).

Halfling Whistler. Req: Wis 13+, Int 10+; Ar: Padded; WPr: Blowgun, short bow, club, light crossbow, dagger, dart, footman's mace, hand axe, harpoon, javelin, knife, quarterstaff, sling, spear, staff sling, short sword, and war hammer. At least half the character's slots must be spent on weapons that can be hurled; NPr: Agriculture (B), dancing (B), spellcraft (B), whistling/humming (B); Races: Halfling (15th level) (M).

9463XXX0502

Bard Spells by Level

Key. Name (School or Element—Ab: Abjuration, A: Alteration, Ch: Charm, C: Conjuration, D: Divination, E: Evocation, EA: Elemental Air; EE: Elemental Earth; EF: Elemental Fire; EW: Elemental Water; En: Enchantment, I: Illusion, In: Invocation; N: Necromancy, P: Phantasm, S: Summoning) Range; Components; Duration (Spcl: Special); Casting Time; Area of Effect; Saving Throw; Book and page number (PH: *Player's Handbook,* TM: *Tome of Magic). Italicized* spells are the reverse of the spell they follow; reverse spells only list spell characteristics different from the normal spell. Lesser Divination school spells are divination spells of fourth level or less.

1st Level

□ □ □ **Affect Normal Fires** (A, EF) R: 5 yd/lvl; C: V,S; D: 2 rd/lvl; CT: 1; AoE: 10′ radius; Save: None; PH131.
□ □ □ **Alarm** (Ab, E) R: 10 yd; C: V,S,M; D: 4 hr+½ hr/lvl; CT: 1 rd; AoE: Up to a 20′ cube; Save: None; PH131.
□ □ □ **Armor** (C) R: Touch; C: V,S,M; D: Spcl; CT: 1 rd; AoE: 1 creature; Save: None; PH131.
□ □ □ **Audible Glamer** (I/P) R: 60 yd+10 yd/lvl; C: V,S,M; D: 3 rd/lvl; CT: 1; AoE: Hearing range; Save: Spcl; PH131.
□ □ □ **Burning Hands** (A, EF) R: 0; C: V,S; D: Instant; CT: 1; AoE: Caster; Save: ½; PH131.
□ □ □ **Cantrip** (All Schools) R: 10 ft; C: V,S; D: 1 hr/lvl; CT: 1; AoE: Spcl; Save: None; PH131.
□ □ □ **Change Self** (I/P) R: 0; C: V,S; D: 2d6 rd+2 rd/lvl; CT: 1; AoE: Caster; Save: None; PH132.
□ □ □ **Charm Person** (En/Ch) R: 120 yd; C: V,S; D: Spcl; CT: 1; AoE: 1 person; Save: Neg; PH132.
□ □ □ **Chill Touch** (N) R: 0; C: V,S; D: 3 rd+1 rd/lvl; CT: 1; AoE: Caster; Save: Neg; PH132.
□ □ □ **Color Spray** (A) R: 0; C: V,S,M; D: Instant; CT: 1; AoE: 5×20×20′ wedge; Save: Spcl; PH132.
□ □ □ **Comprehend Languages** (A) R: Touch; C: V,S,M; D: 5 rd/lvl; CT: 1 rd; AoE: 1 speaking creature or written object; Save: None; PH133.
□ □ □ ***Confuse Languages***
□ □ □ **Conjure Spell Component** (C/S) R: 1 mi/lvl; C: V,S; D: 1 rd; CT: 1; AoE: 3 components/lvl; Save: None; TM17.
□ □ □ **Dancing Lights** (A, EF) R: 40 yd+10 yd/lvl; C: V,S,M; D: 2 rd/lvl; CT: 1; AoE: Spcl; Save: None; PH133.
□ □ □ **Detect Magic** (D) R: 0; C: V,S; D: 2 rd/lvl; CT: 1; AoE: 10′ path, 60′ long; Save: None; PH133.
□ □ □ **Detect Undead** (D, N) R: 0; C: V,S,M; D: 3 tn; CT: 1 rd; AoE: 60′+10′/lvl; Save: None; PH133.
□ □ □ **Enlarge** (A) R: 5 yd/lvl; C: V,S,M; D: 5 rd/lvl; CT: 1; AoE: 1 creature or object; Save: Neg; PH133.
□ □ □ ***Reduce***
□ □ □ **Erase** (A) R: 30 yd; C: V,S; D: Perm; CT: 1; AoE: 1 scroll or 2 pages; Save: Spcl; PH134.
□ □ □ **Feather Fall** (A, EA) R: 10 yd/lvl; C: V; D: 1 rd/lvl; CT: 1; AoE: Spcl; Save: None; PH134.
□ □ □ **Find Familiar** (C/S) R: 1 mi/lvl; C: V,S,M; D: Spcl; CT: 2d12 hr; AoE: 1 familiar; Save: Spcl; PH134.
□ □ □ **Fire Burst** (A, Ev, EF) R: 5 yd/lvl; C: V,S; D: Instant; CT: 1; AoE: 10′-radius circle; Save: Neg; TM17.
□ □ □ **Fist of Stone** (A, EE) R: 0; C: V,S; D: 1 rd/lvl; CT: 1; AoE: Caster's hand; Save: None; TM17.
□ □ □ **Friends** (En/Ch) R: 0; C: V,S,M; D: 1d4 rd+1 rd/lvl; CT: 1; AoE: 60′ radius; Save: Spcl; PH134.
□ □ □ **Gaze Reflection** (A) R: 0; C: V,S; D: 2 rd+1 rd/lvl; CT: 1; AoE: Spcl; Save: None; PH135.
□ □ □ **Grease** (C) R: 10 yd; C: V,S,M; D: 3 rd+1 rd/lvl; CT: 1; AoE: 10×10′ sq area; Save: Spcl; PH135.
□ □ □ **Hold Portal** (A) R: 20 yd/lvl; C: V; D: 1 rd/lvl; CT: 1; AoE: 20 sq ft/lvl; Save: None; PH135.
□ □ □ **Hypnotism** (En/Ch) R: 5 yd; C: V,S; D: 1 rd+1 rd/lvl; CT: 1; AoE: 30′ cube; Save: Neg; PH135.
□ □ □ **Identify** (D) R: 0; C: V,S,M; D: 1 rd/lvl; CT: Spcl; AoE: 1 item/lvl; Save: None; PH135.
□ □ □ **Jump** (A) R: Touch; C: V,S,M; D: 1d3 rd+1 rd/lvl; CT: 1; AoE: Creature touched; Save: None; PH135.
□ □ □ **Lasting Breath** (A, EA) R: 5 yd/lvl; C: V,S; D: 1d4 rd+1 rd/lvl; CT: 1; AoE: 1 creature/lvl; Save: None; TM19.
□ □ □ **Light** (A) R: 60 yd; C: V,M; D: 1 tn/lvl; CT: 1; AoE: 20′ radius; Save: Spcl; PH136.
□ □ □ **Magic Missile** (Ev) R: 60 yd+10 yd/lvl; C: V,S; D: Instant; CT: 1; AoE: 1 or more creatures in a 10′ cube; Save: None; PH136.
□ □ □ **Mending** (A) R: 30 yd; C: V,S,M; D: Perm; CT: 1; AoE: 1 object; Save: None; PH136.
□ □ □ **Message** (A) R: 0; C: V,S,M; D: 5 rd/lvl; CT: 1; AoE: Spcl; Save: None; PH136.
□ □ □ **Metamorphose Liquids** (A, EW) R: Touch; C: V,S,M; D: Perm; CT: 1 rd; AoE: 1′ cube/lvl; Save: Spcl; TM19.
□ □ □ **Mount** (C/S) R: 10 yd; C: V,S,M; D: 2 hr+1 hr/lvl; CT: 1 tn; AoE: 1 mount; Save: None; PH136.
□ □ □ **Murdock's Feathery Flyer** (A) R: 0; C: V,S,M; D: 1 rd/lvl; CT: 1; AoE: Caster; Save: None; TM19.
□ □ □ **Nystul's Magical Aura** (I/P) R: Touch; C: V,S,M; D: 1 d/lvl; CT: 1 rd; AoE: Spcl; Save: Spcl; PH136.
□ □ □ **Phantasmal Force** (I/P) R: 60 yd+10 yd/lvl; C: V,S,M; D: Spcl; CT: 1; AoE: 400 sq ft+100 sq ft/lvl; Save: Spcl; PH137.
□ □ □ **Protection from Evil** (Ab) R: Touch; C: V,S,M; D: 2 rd/lvl; CT: 1; AoE: Creature touched; Save: None; PH137.
□ □ □ ***Protection from Good***
□ □ □ **Read Magic** (D) R: 0; C: V,S,M; D: 2 rd/lvl; CT: 1 rd; AoE: Spcl; Save: None; PH137.
□ □ □ **Shield** (Ev) R: 0; C: V,S; D: 5 rd/lvl; CT: 1; AoE: Spcl; Save: None; PH137.
□ □ □ **Shocking Grasp** (A) R: Touch; C: V,S; D: Spcl; CT: 1; AoE: Creature touched; Save: None; PH137.
□ □ □ **Sleep** (En/Ch) R: 30 yd; C: V,S,M; D: 5 rd/lvl; CT: 1; AoE: Spcl; Save: None; PH138.
□ □ □ **Spider Climb** (A) R: Touch; C: V,S,M; D: 3 rd+1 rd/lvl; CT: 1; AoE: Creature touched; Save: Neg; PH138.
□ □ □ **Spook** (I/P) R: 0; C: V,S; D: Spcl; CT: 1; AoE: 1 creature within 30′; Save: Neg; PH138.
□ □ □ **Taunt** (En) R: 60 yd; C: V,S,M; D: 1 rd; CT: 1; AoE: 30′ radius; Save: Neg; PH138.
□ □ □ **Tenser's Floating Disc** (Ev) R: 20 yd; C: V,S,M; D: 3 tn+1 tn/lvl; CT: 1; AoE: Spcl; Save: None; PH138.
□ □ □ **Unseen Servant** (C/S) R: 0; C: V,S,M; D: 1 hr+1 tn/lvl; CT: 1; AoE: 30′ radius; Save: None; PH138.
□ □ □ **Ventriloquism** (I/P) R: 10 yd/lvl, max 90 yd; C: V,M; D: 4 rd+ 1 rd/lvl; CT: 1; AoE: 1 creature or object; Save: Spcl; PH139.
□ □ □ **Wall of Fog** (Ev, EA) R: 30 yd; C: V,S,M; D: 2d4 rd+1 rd/lvl; CT: 1; AoE: 20′ cube+10′ cube/lvl; Save: None; PH139.
□ □ □ **Wizard Mark** (A) R: Touch; C: V,S,M; D: Perm; CT: 1; AoE: Up to 1 sq ft; Save: None; PH139.

2nd Level

□ □ □ **Alter Self** (A) R: 0; C: V,S; D: 3d4 rd+2 rd/lvl; CT: 2; AoE: Caster; Save: None; PH139.
□ □ □ **Bind** (En) R: 30 yd; C: V,S,M; D: 1 rd/lvl; CT: 2; AoE: Spcl; Save: None; PH139.
□ □ □ **Blindness** (I/P) R: 30 yd+ 10 yd/lvl; C: V; D: Spcl; CT: 2; AoE: 1 creature; Save: Neg; PH140.
□ □ □ **Blur** (I/P) R: 0; C: V,S; D: 3 rd+1 rd/lvl; CT: 2; AoE: Caster; Save: None; PH140.
□ □ □ **Continual Light** (A) R: 60 yd; C: V,S; D: Perm; CT: 2; AoE: 60′ radius; Save: Spcl; PH140.
□ □ □ ***Continual Darkness***
□ □ □ **Darkness, 15′ Radius** (A) R: 10 yd/lvl; C: V,S,M; D: 1 tn+1 rd/lvl; CT: 2; AoE: 15′ radius; Save: None; PH140.
□ □ □ **Deafness** (I/P) R: 60 yd; C: V,S,M; D: Spcl; CT: 2; AoE: 1 creature; Save: Neg; PH140.
□ □ □ **Deeppockets** (A, En) R: Touch; C: V,S,M; D: 12 hr+1 hr/lvl; CT: 1 tn; AoE: 1 garment; Save: None; PH140.
□ □ □ **Detect Evil** (D) R: 60 yd; C: V,S; D: 5 rd/lvl; CT: 2; AoE: 10′ path; Save: None; PH140.
□ □ □ ***Detect Good***
□ □ □ **Detect Invisibility** (D) R: 10 yd/lvl; C: V,S,M; D: 5 rd/lvl; CT: 2; AoE: 10′ path; Save: None; PH141.
□ □ □ **ESP** (D) R: 5 yd/lvl, 90 yd max; C: V,S,M; D: 1 rd/lvl; CT: 2; AoE: 1 creature per probe; Save: None; PH141.
□ □ □ **Flaming Sphere** (Ev, EF) R: 10 yd; C: V,S,M; D: 1 rd/lvl; CT: 2; AoE: 3′ radius; Save: Neg; PH141.
□ □ □ **Fog Cloud** (A, EA) R: 10 yd C: V,S; D: 4 rd+1 rd/lvl; CT: 2; AoE: Spcl; Save: None; PH141.
□ □ □ **Fools' Gold** (A, I, EE) R: 10 yd; C: V,S,M; D: 1 hr/lvl; CT: 1 rd; AoE: 10 cu in/lvl; Save: Spcl; PH141.
□ □ □ **Forget** (En/Ch) R: 30 yd; C: V,S; D: Perm; CT: 2; AoE: 20′ cube; Save: Neg; PH142.
□ □ □ **Glitterdust** (C/S) R: 10 yd/lvl; C: V,S,M; D: Spcl; CT: 2; AoE: 20′ cube; Save: Spcl; PH142.
□ □ □ **Hypnotic Pattern** (I/P) R: 30 yd; C: S,M; D: Spcl; CT: 2; AoE: 30′ cube; Save: Neg; PH142.
□ □ □ **Improved Phantasmal Force** (I/P) R: 60 yd+10 yd/lvl; C: V,S,M; D: Spcl; CT: 2; AoE: 200 sq ft+50 sq ft/lvl; Save: Spcl; PH142.

Bard Spells by Level (con't)

☐☐☐ **Insatiable Thirst** (En/Ch, EW) R: 5 yd/lvl; C: V,S; D: 1 rd/lvl; CT: 2; AoE: 1 creature; Save: Neg; TM21.
☐☐☐ **Invisibility** (I/P) R: Touch; C: V,S,M; D: Spcl; CT: 2; AoE: Creature touched; Save: None; PH142.
☐☐☐ **Irritation** (A) R: 10 yd/lvl; C: V,S,M; D: Spcl; CT: 2; AoE: 1–4 creatures in a 15′ radius; Save: Neg; PH142.
☐☐☐ **Knock** (A) R: 60 yd; C: V; D: Spcl; CT: 1; AoE: 10 sq ft/lvl; Save: None; PH143.
  ☐☐☐ ***Lock***
☐☐☐ **Know Alignment** (D) R: 10 yd; C: V,S; D: 1 rd/lvl; CT: 1 rd; AoE: 1 creature or object per 2 rd; Save: Neg; PH143.
  ☐☐☐ ***Undetectable Alignment*** D: 24 hr; AoE: 1 creature or object; Save: None.
☐☐☐ **Leomund's Trap** (I/P) R: Touch; C: V,S,M; D: Perm; CT: 3 rd; AoE: Object touched; Save: None; PH143.
☐☐☐ **Levitate** (A) R: 20 yd/lvl; C: V,S,M; D: 1 tn/lvl; CT: 2; AoE: 1 creature or object; Save: Neg; PH143.
☐☐☐ **Locate Object** (D) R: 20 yd/lvl; C: V,S,M; D: 1 rd/lvl; CT: 2; AoE: Spcl; Save: None; PH143.
  ☐☐☐ ***Obscure Object*** D: 8 hr; AoE: 1 object.
☐☐☐ **Magic Mouth** (A) R: 10 yd; C: V,S,M; D: Spcl; CT: 2; AoE: 1 object; Save: None; PH143.
☐☐☐ **Maximilian's Earthen Grasp** (A, EE) R: 10 yd+10 yd/lvl; C: V,S,M; D: 3 rd+1 rd/lvl; CT: 2; AoE: 1 creature; Save: Spcl; TM22.
☐☐☐ **Melf's Acid Arrow** (C) R: 180 yd; C: V,S,M; D: Spcl; CT: 2; AoE: 1 target; Save: Spcl; PH144.
☐☐☐ **Mirror Image** (I/P) R: 0; C: V,S; D: 3 rd/lvl; CT: 2; AoE: 6′ radius; Save: None; PH144.
☐☐☐ **Misdirection** (I/P) R: 30 yd; C: V,S; D: 8 hr; CT: 2; AoE: 1 creature or object; Save: Neg; PH144.
☐☐☐ **Past Life** (D) R: Touch; C: V,S; D: Spcl; CT: 1 rd; AoE: 1 creature; Save: None; TM22.
☐☐☐ **Protection from Cantrips** (Ab) R: Touch; C: V,S; D: 5 hr+1 hr/lvl; CT: 1 rd; AoE: Creature or object touched; Save: None; PH144.
☐☐☐ **Protection from Paralysis** (Ab) R: Touch; C: V,S,M; D: 1 tn/lvl; CT: 2; AoE: 1 creature; Save: None; TM23.
☐☐☐ **Pyrotechnics** (A, EF) R: 120 yd; C: V,S,M; D: Spcl; CT: 2; AoE: 1 fire source (spcl); Save: Spcl; PH144.
☐☐☐ **Ray of Enfeeblement** (En/Ch) R: 10 yd+5 yd/lvl; C: V,S; D: 1 rd/lvl; CT: 2; AoE: 1 creature; Save: Neg; PH145.
☐☐☐ **Ride the Wind** (A, EA) R: 5 yd/lvl; C: V,S,M; D: 1 tn/lvl; CT: 2; AoE: 1 creature/lvl; Save: Neg; TM23.
☐☐☐ **Rope Trick** (A) R: Touch; C: V,S,M; D: 2 tn/lvl; CT: 2; AoE: Spcl; Save: None; PH145.
☐☐☐ **Scare** (En/Ch) R: 30 yd+10 yd/lvl; C: V,S,M; D: 1d4 rd+1 rd/lvl; CT: 2; AoE: 15′ radius; Save: Spcl; PH145.
☐☐☐ **Sense Shifting** (A) R: 0; C: V,S,M; D: 3 tn; CT: 2; AoE: Caster; Save: None; TM23.
☐☐☐ **Shatter** (A) R: 30 yd+10 yd/lvl; C: V,S,M; D: Instant; CT: 2; AoE: 3′ radius; Save: Neg; PH145.
☐☐☐ **Spectral Hand** (N) R: 30 yd+5 yd/lvl; C: V,S; D: 2 rd/lvl; CT: 2; AoE: 1 opponent; Save: None; PH145.
☐☐☐ **Stinking Cloud** (Ev, EA) R: 30 yd; C: V,S,M; D: 1 rd/lvl; CT: 2; AoE: 20′ cube; Save: Spcl; PH145.
☐☐☐ **Strength** (A) R: Touch; C: V,S,M; D: 1 hr/lvl; CT: 1 tn; AoE: Person touched; Save: None; PH146.
☐☐☐ **Summon Swarm** (C/S) R: 60 yd; C: V,S,M; D: Spcl; CT: 2; AoE: 10′ cube; Save: Neg; PH146.
☐☐☐ **Tasha's Uncontrollable Hideous Laughter** (En/Ch) R: 60 yd; C: V,S,M; D: 1 rd/lvl; CT: 2; AoE: 1 or more creatures in a 30′ cube; Save: Neg; PH146.
☐☐☐ **Web** (Ev) R: 5 yd/lvl; C: V,S,M; D: 2 tn/lvl; CT: 2; AoE: Spcl; Save: Neg or ½; PH146.
☐☐☐ **Whispering Wind** (A, P, EA) R: 1 mi/lvl; C: V,S; D: Spcl; CT: 1; AoE: 2′ radius; Save: None; PH147.
☐☐☐ **Wizard Lock** (A) R: Touch; C: V,S; D: Perm; CT: 2; AoE: 30 sq ft/lvl; Save: None; PH147.

3rd Level

☐☐☐ **Alacrity** (A) R: 0; C: V,S,M; D: 1 tn+1 rd/lvl; CT: 1; AoE: Caster; Save: None; TM24.
☐☐☐ **Alamir's Fundamental Breakdown** (D, EA, EE, EF, EW) R: Touch; C: V,S,M; D: Spcl; CT: 1 rd; AoE: 1 item; Save: Spcl; TM24.
☐☐☐ **Augmentation I** (In/Ev) R: 0; C: V,S,M; D: Spcl; CT: 2; AoE: Spcl; Save: None; TM25.
☐☐☐ **Blink** (A) R: 0; C: V,S; D: 1 rd/lvl; CT: 1; AoE: Caster; Save: None; PH147.
☐☐☐ **Clairaudience** (D) R: Spcl; C: V,S,M; D: 1 rd/lvl; CT: 3; AoE: Spcl; Save: None; PH147.
☐☐☐ **Clairvoyance** (D) R: Spcl; C: V,S,M; D: 1 rd/lvl; CT: 3; AoE: Spcl; Save: None; PH147.
☐☐☐ **Delude** (A) R: 0; C: V,S; D: 1 tn/lvl; CT: 3; AoE: Caster; Save: Neg; PH148.
☐☐☐ **Dispel Magic** (Ab) R: 120 yd; C: V,S; D: Instant; CT: 3; AoE: 30′ cube; Save: None; PH148.
☐☐☐ **Explosive Runes** (A) R: Touch; C: V,S; D: Spcl; CT: 3; AoE: 10′ radius; Save: None or ½; PH148.
☐☐☐ **Far Reaching I** (A) R: 0; C: V; D: Spcl; CT: 2; AoE: Spcl; Save: None; TM25.
☐☐☐ **Feign Death** (N) R: Touch; C: V,S; D: 1 hr+1 tn/lvl; CT: 1; AoE: Creature touched; Save: None; PH149.
☐☐☐ **Fireball** (Ev, EF) R: 10 yd+10 yd/lvl; C: V,S,M; D: Instant; CT: 3; AoE: 20′ radius; Save: ½; PH149.
☐☐☐ **Flame Arrow** (C/S, EF) R: 30 yd+10 yd/lvl; C: V,S,M; D: 1 rd; CT: 3; AoE: Spcl; Save: None; PH149.
☐☐☐ **Fly** (A) R: Touch; C: V,S,M; D: 1 tn/lvl+1d6 tn; CT: 3; AoE: Creature touched; Save: None; PH149.
☐☐☐ **Gust of Wind** (A, EA) R: 0; C: V,S,M; D: 1 rd; CT: 3; AoE: 10′-wide path, 10 yd/lvl long; Save: None; PH149.
☐☐☐ **Haste** (A) R: 60 yd; C: V,S,M; D: 3 rd+1 rd/lvl; CT: 3; AoE: 40′ cube, 1 creature/lvl; Save: None; PH149.
☐☐☐ **Hold Person** (En/Ch) R: 120 yd; C: V,S,M; D: 2 rd/lvl; CT: 3; AoE: 1d4 persons in a 20′ cube; Save: Neg; PH150.
☐☐☐ **Hold Undead** (N) R: 20 yd; C: V,S,M; D: 1d4 rd+1 rd/lvl; CT: 5; AoE: 1d3 undead; Save: Neg; PH150.
☐☐☐ **Illusionary Script** (I/P) R: Touch; C: V,S,M; D: 1 day/lvl; CT: Spcl; AoE: Creature reading the script; Save: Spcl; PH150.
☐☐☐ **Infravision** (A) R: Touch; C: V,S,M; D: 2 hr+1hr/lvl; CT: 1 rd; AoE: Creature touched; Save: None; PH150.
☐☐☐ **Invisibility, 10′ Radius** (I/P) R: Touch; C: V,S,M; D: Spcl; CT: 3; AoE: 10′ radius of creature touched; Save: None; PH150.
☐☐☐ **Item** (A) R: Touch; C: V,S,M; D: 4 hr/lvl; CT: 3; AoE: 2 cu ft/lvl; Save: Spcl; PH150.
☐☐☐ **Leomund's Tiny Hut** (A) R: 0; C: V,S,M; D: 4 hr+1hr/lvl; CT: 3; AoE: 15′ diam; Save: None; PH151.
☐☐☐ **Lightning Bolt** (Ev) R: 40 yd+10 yd/lvl; C: V,S,M; D: Instant; CT: 3; AoE: Spcl; Save: ½; PH151.
☐☐☐ **Lorloveim's Creeping Shadow** (I) R: 0; C: V,S,M; D: 1 rd/lvl; CT: 7; AoE: Caster's shadow; Save: None; TM26.
☐☐☐ **Maximilian's Stony Grasp** (A, EE) R: 20 yd+10 yd/lvl; C: V,S,M; D: 5 rd+1 rd/lvl; CT: 3; AoE: 1 creature; Save: Spcl; TM26.
☐☐☐ **Melf's Minute Meteors** (Ev, A, EF) R: 70 yd+10 yd/lvl; C: V,S,M; D: Spcl; CT: 3; AoE: 1 target per meteor; Save: None; PH151.
☐☐☐ **Minor Malison** (En/Ch) R: 20 yd; C: V; D: 2 rd/lvl; CT: 2; AoE: 30′ radius; Save: None; TM26.
☐☐☐ **Monster Summoning I** (C/S) R: 30 yd; C: V,S,M; D: 2 rd+1 rd/lvl; CT: 3; AoE: Spcl; Save: None; PH151.
☐☐☐ **Non-Detection** (Ab) R: Touch; C: V,S,M; D: 1 hr/lvl; CT: 3; AoE: 1 creature or item; Save: None; PH152.
☐☐☐ **Phantom Steed** (C, P) R: Touch; C: V,S; D: 1 hr/lvl; CT: 1 tn; AoE: Spcl; Save: None; PH152.
☐☐☐ **Protection from Evil, 10′ Radius** (Ab) R: Touch; C: V,S,M; D: 2 rd/lvl; CT: 3; AoE: 10′ radius around creature touched; Save: None; PH152.
  ☐☐☐ ***Protection from Good, 10′ Radius***
☐☐☐ **Protection from Normal Missiles** (Ab) R: Touch; C: V,S,M; D: 1 tn/lvl; CT: 3; AoE: Creature touched; Save: None; PH152.
☐☐☐ **Secret Page** (A) R: Touch; C: V,S,M; D: Until dispelled; CT: 1 tn; AoE: 1 page of any size, up to 2 ft sq; Save: None; PH152.
☐☐☐ **Sepia Snake Sigil** (C/S) R: 5 yd; C: V,S,M; D: Spcl; CT: 3; AoE: 1 sigil; Save: None; PH152.
☐☐☐ **Slow** (A) R: 90 yd+10 yd/lvl; C: V,S,M; D: 3 rd+1 rd/lvl; CT: 3; AoE: 40′ cube, 1 creature/lvl; Save: Neg; PH153.
☐☐☐ **Spectral Force** (I/P) R: 60 yd+1 yd/lvl; C: V,S; D: Spcl; CT: 3; AoE: 40′ cube+a 10′ cube/lvl; Save: Spcl; PH153.
☐☐☐ **Spirit Armor** (N) R: 0; C: V,S; D: 2 rd/lvl; CT: 3; AoE: Caster; Save: Spcl; TM26.
☐☐☐ **Squaring the Circle** (A) R: 0; C: V,S,M; D: 1 rd/lvl; CT: 2; AoE: Spcl; Save: None; TM27.
☐☐☐ **Suggestion** (En/Ch) R: 30 yd; C: V,M; D: 1 hr+1 hr/lvl; CT: 3; AoE: 1 creature; Save: Neg; PH153.
☐☐☐ **Tongues** (A) R: 0; C: V,M; D: 1 rd/lvl; CT: 3; AoE: 30′ radius; Save: None; PH153.
  ☐☐☐ ***Babble***
☐☐☐ **Vampiric Touch** (N) R: 0; C: V,S; D: 1 touch; CT: 3; AoE: Caster; Save: None; PH153.
☐☐☐ **Water Breathing** (A, EA, EW) R: Touch; C: V,S,M; D: 1 hr/lvl+1d4 hr; CT: 3; AoE: Creature touched; Save: None; PH153.
  ☐☐☐ ***Air Breathing***

Bard Spells by Level (con't)

☐☐☐ **Watery Double** (C/S, En, EW) R: Touch; C: V,S; D: Spcl, max 10 rd; CT: 3; AoE: 1 body of liquid; Save: Neg; TM27.
☐☐☐ **Wind Wall** (A, EA) R: 10 yd/lvl; C: V,S,M; D: 1 rd/lvl; CT: 3; AoE: a 10′ wide × 5′ high area/lvl; Save: Spcl; PH154.
☐☐☐ **Wizard Sight** (D) R: 0; C: V,S; D: 1 rd/lvl; CT: 3; AoE: Caster; Save: None; TM28.
☐☐☐ **Wraithform** (A, I) R: 0; C: S,M; D: 2 rd/lvl; CT: 1; AoE: Caster; Save: None; PH154.

4th Level

☐☐☐ **Charm Monster** (En/Ch) R: 60 yd; C: V,S; D: Spcl; CT: 4; AoE: 1 or more creatures in a 20′ radius; Save: Neg; PH154.
☐☐☐ **Confusion** (En/Ch) R: 120 yd; C: V,S,M; D: 2 rd+1 rd/lvl; CT: 4; AoE: Up to 60′ cube; Save: Spcl; PH154.
☐☐☐ **Contagion** (N) R: 30 yd; C: V,S; D: Perm; CT: 4; AoE: 1 creature; Save: Neg; PH155.
☐☐☐ **Detect Scrying** (D) R: 0; C: V,S,M; D: 1d6 tn+1 tn/lvl; CT: 3; AoE: 120′ radius; Save: Spcl; PH155.
☐☐☐ **Dig** (Ev, EE) R: 30 yd; C: V,S,M; D: 1 rd/lvl; CT: 4; AoE: 5′ cube/lvl; Save: Spcl; PH155.
☐☐☐ **Dilation I** (A) R: 0 C: V; D: Spcl; CT: 4; AoE: Spcl; Save: None; TM28.
☐☐☐ **Dimension Door** (A) R: 0; C: V; D: Instant; CT: 1; AoE: Caster; Save: None; PH155.
☐☐☐ **Divination Enhancement** (Ev) R: 0; C: V; D: 2 tn+2 rd/lvl; CT: 4; AoE: Caster; Save: None; TM28.
☐☐☐ **Emotion** (En/Ch) R: 10 yd/lvl; C: V,S; D: Spcl; CT: 4; AoE: 20′ cube; Save: Neg; PH155.
☐☐☐ **Enchanted Weapon** (En) R: Touch; C: V,S,M; D: 5 rd/lvl; CT: 1 tn; AoE: Weapon(s) touched; Save: None; PH157.
☐☐☐ **Enervation** (N) R: 10 yd/lvl; C: V,S; D: 1d4 hr+1 hr/lvl; CT: 4; AoE: 1 creature; Save: Neg; PH157.
☐☐☐ **Evard's Black Tentacles** (C/S) R: 30 yd; C: V,S,M; D: 1 hr/lvl; CT: 1 rd; AoE: 30 sq ft/lvl; Save: None; PH157.
☐☐☐ **Extension I** (A) R: 0 C: V; D: Spcl; CT: 2; AoE: Spcl; Save: None; PH157.
☐☐☐ **Far Reaching II** (A) R: 0; C: V; D: Spcl; CT: 4; AoE: Spcl; Save: None; TM28.
☐☐☐ **Fear** (I/P) R: 0; C: V,S,M; D: Spcl; CT: 4; AoE: 60′ long cone, 30′ diam at end, 5′ at base; Save: Neg; PH157.
☐☐☐ **Fire Charm** (En/Ch, EF) R: 10 yd; C: V,S,M; D: 2 rd/lvl; CT: 4; AoE: 15′ radius of fire; Save: Neg; PH158.
☐☐☐ **Fire Shield** (Ev, A, EF) R: 0; C: V,S,M; D: 2 rd+1 rd/lvl; CT: 4; AoE: Caster; Save: None; PH158.
☐☐☐ **Fire Trap** (Ab, Ev, EF) R: Touch; C: V,S,M; D: Perm until discharged; CT: 1 tn; AoE: Object touched; Save: ½; PH158.
☐☐☐ **Fumble** (En/Ch) R: 10 yd/lvl; C: V,S,M; D: 1 rd/lvl; CT: 4; AoE: 30′ cube; Save: Spcl; PH158.
☐☐☐ **Greater Malison** (En/Ch) R: 20 yd; C: V; D: 2 rd/lvl; CT: 4; AoE: 30′ radius; Save: None; TM29.
☐☐☐ **Hallucinatory Terrain** (I/P) R: 20 yd/lvl; C: V,S,M; D: 1 hr/lvl; CT: 1 tn; AoE: Cube up to 30′ per side/lvl; Save: None; PH158.
☐☐☐ **Ice Storm** (Ev, EW) R: 10 yd/lvl; C: V,S,M; D: Spcl; CT: 4; AoE: Spcl; Save: None; PH159.
☐☐☐ **Illusionary Wall** (I/P) R: 30 yd; C: V,S; D: Perm; CT: 4; AoE: 1×10×10′; Save: None; PH159.
☐☐☐ **Improved Invisibility** (I/P) R: Touch; C: V,S; D: 4 rd+1 rd/lvl; CT: 4; AoE: Creature touched; Save: None; PH159.
☐☐☐ **Leomund's Secure Shelter** (A, En) R: 20 yd; C: V,S,M; D: 1d4+1 hr+1 hr/lvl; CT: 4 tn; AoE: 30 sq ft/lvl; Save: None; PH159.
☐☐☐ **Locate Creature** (D) R: 50 yd/lvl; C: V,S,M; D: 1 tn/lvl; CT: 5; AoE: 1 creature; Save: None; TM29.
☐☐☐ **Magic Mirror** (En, D) R: Touch; C: V,S,M; D: 1 rd/lvl; CT: 1 hr; AoE: Spcl; Save: None; PH159.
☐☐☐ **Mask of Death** (N) R: Touch; C: V,S,M; D: 1 hr/lvl; CT: 1 rd; AoE: 1 creature; Save: None; TM29.
☐☐☐ **Massmorph** (A) R: 10 yd/lvl; C: V,S,M; D: Spcl; CT: 4; AoE: 1 10′ cube/lvl; Save: None; PH160.
☐☐☐ **Minor Creation** (I/P) R: Touch; C: V,S,M; D: 1 hr/lvl; CT: 1 tn; AoE: Spcl; Save: None; PH160.
☐☐☐ **Minor Globe of Invulnerability** (Ab) R: 0; C: V,S,M; D: 1 rd/lvl; CT: 4; AoE: 5′ radius; Save: None; PH160.
☐☐☐ **Minor Spell Turning** (Ab) R: 0; C: V,S,M; D: 3 rd/lvl; CT: 4; AoE: Caster; Save: None; TM29.
☐☐☐ **Monster Summoning II** (C/S) R: 40 yd; C: V,S,M; D: 3 rd+1 rd/lvl; CT: 4; AoE: Spcl; Save: None; PH160.
☐☐☐ **Mordenkainen's Celerity** (A, In) R: 0; C: V,S,M; D: 1 tn; CT: 4; AoE: Spcl; Save: None; TM30.
☐☐☐ **Otiluke's Resilient Sphere** (A, Ev) R: 20 yd; C: V,S,M; D: 1 rd/lvl; CT: 4; AoE: 1′ diam/lvl; Save: Neg; PH160.
☐☐☐ **Phantasmal Killer** (I/P) R: 5 yd/lvl; C: V,S; D: 1 rd/lvl; CT: 4; AoE: 1 creature; Save: Spcl; PH160.
☐☐☐ **Plant Growth** (A) R: 10 yd/lvl; C: V,S; D: Perm; CT: 4; AoE: An area 10′ per side/lvl; Save: None; PH161.
☐☐☐ **Polymorph Other** (A) R: 5 yd/lvl; C: V,S,M; D: Perm; CT: 4; AoE: 1 creature; Save: Neg; PH161.
☐☐☐ **Polymorph Self** (A) R: 0; C: V; D: 2 tn/lvl; CT: 4; AoE: Caster; Save: None; PH161.
☐☐☐ **Rainbow Pattern** (A, I/P) R: 10 yd; C: S,M; D: Spcl; CT: 4; AoE: 30′ cube; Save: Neg; PH162.
☐☐☐ **Rary's Mnemonic Enhancer** (A) R: 0; C: V,S,M; D: 1 day; CT: 1 tn; AoE: Caster; Save: None; PH162.
☐☐☐ **Remove Curse** (Ab) R: Touch; C: V,S; D: Perm; CT: 4; AoE: Spcl; Save: Spcl; PH162.
 ☐☐☐ *Bestow Curse* D: 1 tn/lvl; Save: Neg.
☐☐☐ **Shadow Monsters** (I/P) R: 30 yd; C: V,S; D: 1 rd/lvl; CT: 4; AoE: 20′ cube; Save: Spcl; PH162.
☐☐☐ **Shout** (Ev) R: 0; C: V,M; D: Instant; CT: 1; AoE: 10×30′ cone; Save: Spcl; PH163.
☐☐☐ **Solid Fog** (A, EA) R: 30 yd; C: V,S,M; D: 2d4 rd+1 rd/lvl; CT: 4; AoE: 20×10×10′ volume/lvl; Save: None; PH163.
☐☐☐ **Stoneskin** (A, EE) R: Touch; C: V,S,M; D: Spcl; CT: 1; AoE: 1 creature; Save: None; PH163.
☐☐☐ **Summon Lycanthrope** (C/S) R: Spcl; C: V,S,M; D: Spcl; CT: 1 tn; AoE: 1 creature; Save: Neg; TM30.
☐☐☐ **Thunder Staff** (In/Ev) R: 0; C: V,S,M; D: Instant; CT: 4; AoE: 20×40′ cone; Save: ½; TM32.
☐☐☐ **Turn Pebble to Boulder** (A, EE) R: Touch; C: V,S,M; D: Spcl; CT: 4; AoE: Spcl; Save: None; TM33.
 ☐☐☐ *Turn Boulder to Pebble* D: Until dispelled.
☐☐☐ **Vacancy** (A, I/P) R: 10 yd/lvl; C: V,S,M; D: 1 hr/lvl; CT: 4; AoE: 10′ radius/lvl; Save: None; PH163.
☐☐☐ **Wall of Fire** (Ev, EF) R: 60 yd; C: V,S,M; D: Spcl; CT: 4; AoE: Spcl; Save: None; PH163.
☐☐☐ **Wall of Ice** (Ev, EW) R: 10 yd/lvl; C: V,S,M; D: 1 tn/lvl; CT: 4; AoE: Spcl; Save: None; PH164.
☐☐☐ **Wizard Eye** (A) R: 0; C: V,S,M; D: 1 rd/lvl; CT: 1 tn; AoE: Spcl; Save: None; PH164.

5th Level

☐☐☐ **Advanced Illusion** (I/P) R: 60 yd+10 yd/lvl; C: V,S,M; D: 1 rd/lvl; CT: 1 rd; AoE: 1 40′ cube+a 10′ cube/lvl; Save: Spcl; PH164.
☐☐☐ **Airy Water** (A, EA, EW) R: 0; C: V,S,M; D: 1 tn/lvl; CT: 5; AoE: 10′ radius sphere or 15′ radius hemisphere; Save: None; PH165.
☐☐☐ **Animal Growth** (A) R: 60 yd; C: V,S,M; D: 1 rd/lvl; CT: 5; AoE: Up to 8 animals in a 20′ cube; Save: None; PH165.
 ☐☐☐ *Shrink Animal*
☐☐☐ **Animate Dead** (N) R: 10 yd; C: V,S,M; D: Perm; CT: 5 rd; AoE: Spcl; Save: None; PH165.
☐☐☐ **Avoidance** (Ab, A) R: 10 yd; C: V,S,M; D: Perm until dispelled; CT: 5; AoE: Up to a 3′ cube; Save: Spcl; PH165.
 ☐☐☐ *Attraction*
☐☐☐ **Bigby's Interposing Hand** (Ev) R: 10 yd/lvl; C: V,S,M; D: 1 rd/lvl; CT: 5; AoE: Spcl; Save: None; PH165.
☐☐☐ **Chaos** (En/Ch) R: 5 yd/lvl; C: V,S,M; D: 1 rd/lvl; CT: 5; AoE: Up to 40′ cube; Save: Spcl; PH166.
☐☐☐ **Cloudkill** (Ev, EA) R: 10 yd; C: V,S; D: 1 rd/lvl; CT: 5; AoE: 40×20×20′ cloud; Save: None; PH166.
☐☐☐ **Cone of Cold** (Ev, EW) R: 0; C: V,S,M; D: Instant; CT: 5; AoE: Spcl; Save: ½; PH166.
☐☐☐ **Conjure Elemental** (C/S, EA, EE, EF, EW) R: 60 yd; C: V,S,M; D: 1 tn/lvl; CT: 1 tn; AoE: Spcl; Save: None; PH166.
☐☐☐ **Contact Other Plane** (D) R: 0; C: V; D: Spcl; CT: 1 tn; AoE: Spcl; Save: None; PH167.
☐☐☐ **Demi-Shadow Monsters** (I/P) R: 30 yd; C: V,S; D: 1 rd/lvl; CT: 5; AoE: 20′ cube; Save: Spcl; PH167.
☐☐☐ **Dismissal** (Ab) R: 10 yd; C: V,S,M; D: Perm; CT: 1 rd; AoE: 1 creature; Save: Neg; PH167.
☐☐☐ **Distance Distortion** (A, EE) R: 10 yd/lvl; C: V,S,M; D: 2 tn/lvl; CT: 5; AoE: One 10′ cube/lvl; Save: None; PH167.
☐☐☐ **Domination** (En/Ch) R: 10 yd/lvl; C: V,S; D: Spcl; CT: 5; AoE: 1 person; Save: Neg; PH168.
☐☐☐ **Dream** (In, I/P) R: Touch; C: V,S; D: Spcl; CT: 1 tn; AoE: 1 creature; Save: None; PH168.
 ☐☐☐ *Nightmare* Save: Neg.

Bard Spells by Level (con't)

□ □ □ **Extension II** (A) R: 0; C: V; D: Spcl; CT: 4; AoE: Spcl; Save: None; PH168.
□ □ □ **Fabricate** (En, A) R: 5 yd/lvl; C: V,S,M; D: Perm; CT: Spcl; AoE: 1 cu yd/lvl; Save: None; PH168.
□ □ □ **False Vision** (D) R: 0; C: V,S,M; D: 1d4 rd+1 rd/lvl; CT: 5; AoE: 30′ radius; Save: None; PH168.
□ □ □ **Far Reaching III** (A) R: 0; C: V; D: Spcl; CT: 5; AoE: Spcl; Save: None; TM34.
□ □ □ **Feeblemind** (En/Ch) R: 10 yd/lvl; C: V,S,M; D: Perm; CT: 5; AoE: 1 creature; Save: Neg; PH168.
□ □ □ **Hold Monster** (En/Ch) R: 5 yd/lvl; C: V,S,M; D: 1 rd/lvl; CT: 5; AoE: 1–4 creatures in a 40′ cube; Save: Neg; PH169.
□ □ □ **Khazid's Procurement** (D, S) R: Spcl; C: V,S,M; D: 1 rd/lvl; CT: 1 tn; AoE: Spcl; Save: None; TM34.
□ □ □ **Leomund's Lamentable Belaborment** (En, Ev) R: 10 yd; C: V; D: Spcl; CT: 5; AoE: 1 or more creatures in a 10′ radius; Save: Spcl; PH169.
□ □ □ **Leomund's Secret Chest** (A, C/S) R: Spcl; C: V,S,M; D: 60 d; CT: 1 tn; AoE: 1 chest of about 2×2×3′ size; Save: None; PH169.
□ □ □ **Lower Resistance** (Ab, A) R: 60 yd; C: V,S,M; D: 1 tn+1 rd/lvl; CT: 5; AoE: 1 creature; Save: None; TM34.
□ □ □ **Magic Jar** (N) R: 10 yd/lvl; C: V,S,M; D: Spcl; CT: 1 rd; AoE: 1 creature; Save: Spcl; PH169.
□ □ □ **Magic Staff** (En/Ch) R: Touch; C: V,S,M; D: Spcl; CT: Spcl; AoE: Caster's staff; Save: None; TM35.
□ □ □ **Major Creation** (I/P) R: 10 yd; C: V,S,M; D: Spcl; CT: 1 tn; AoE: Spcl; Save: None; PH170.
□ □ □ **Mind Fog** (En/Ch) R: 80 yd; C: V,S; D: 3 tn; CT: 3; AoE: 20′ cube; Save: Neg; TM35.
□ □ □ **Monster Summoning III** (C/S) R: 50 yd; C: V,S,M; D: 4 rd+1 rd/lvl; CT: 5; AoE: Spcl; Save: None; PH170.
□ □ □ **Mordenkainen's Faithful Hound** (C/S) R: 10 yd; C: V,S,M; D: Spcl; CT: 5; AoE: Spcl; Save: None; PH170.
□ □ □ **Passwall** (A, EE) R: 30 yd; C: V,S,M; D: 1 hr+1 tn/lvl; CT: 5; AoE: Spcl; Save: None; PH171.
□ □ □ **Safeguarding** (Ab) R: 0; C: V,S,M; D: 1 tn+1 tn/lvl; CT: 5; AoE: 15′ radius; Save: None; TM35.
□ □ □ **Seeming** (I/P) R: 10′ radius; C: V,S; D: 12 hr; CT: 5; AoE: 1 person/2 lvl; Save: None; PH171.
□ □ □ **Sending** (Ev) R: Spcl; C: V,S,M; D: Spcl; CT: 1 tn; AoE: 1 creature; Save: None; PH171.
□ □ □ **Shadow Door** (I/P) R: 10 yd; C: S; D: 1 rd/lvl; CT: 2; AoE: Spcl; Save: None; PH171.
□ □ □ **Shadow Magic** (I/P) R: 50 yd+10 yd/lvl; C: V,S; D: Spcl; CT: 5; AoE: Spcl; Save: Spcl; PH171.
□ □ □ **Stone Shape** (A, EE) R: Touch; C: V,S,M; D: Perm; CT: 1 rd; AoE: 1 cu ft/lvl; Save: None; PH171.
□ □ □ **Summon Shadow** (C/S, N) R: 10 yd; C: V,S,M; D: 1 rd+1 rd/lvl; CT: 5; AoE: 10′ cube; Save: None; PH171.
□ □ □ **Telekinesis** (A) R: 10 yd/lvl; C: V,S; D: Spcl; CT: 5; AoE: Spcl; Save: Neg; PH171.
□ □ □ **Teleport** (A) R: Touch; C: V; D: Instant; CT: 2; AoE: Spcl; Save: None; PH172.
□ □ □ **Transmute Rock to Mud** (A, EE, EW) R: 10 yd/lvl; C: V,S,M; D: Spcl; CT: 5; AoE: 1 20′ cube/lvl; Save: None; PH172.
  □ □ □ ***Transmute Mud to Rock***
□ □ □ **Von Gasik's Refusal** (Ab) R: 10 yd/lvl; C: V,S,M; D: 1 hr/lvl; CT: 5; AoE: 20′ sq/lvl; Save: None; TM36.
□ □ □ **Wall of Force** (Ev) R: 30 yd; C: V,S,M; D: 1 tn+1 rd/lvl; CT: 5; AoE: Up to 10′ sq/lvl; Save: None; PH172.
□ □ □ **Wall of Iron** (Ev, EE) R: 5 yd/lvl; C: V,S,M; D: Perm; CT: 5; AoE: 15 sq ft/lvl or spcl; Save: None; PH172.
□ □ □ **Wall of Stone** (Ev, EE) R: 5 yd/lvl; C: V,S,M; D: Perm; CT: 5; AoE: Spcl; Save: None; PH173.

6th Level

□ □ □ **Anti-Magic Shell** (Ab) R: 0; C: V,S; D: 1 tn/lvl; CT: 1; AoE: 1′/lvl-diam sphere; Save: None; PH173.
□ □ □ **Augmentation II** (Ev) R: 0; C: V,S,M; D: 3 tn; CT: 6; AoE: Spcl; Save: None; TM37.
□ □ □ **Bigby's Forceful Hand** (Ev) R: 10 yd/lvl; C: V,S,M; D: 1 rd/lvl; CT: 6; AoE: Spcl; Save: None; PH173.
□ □ □ **Bloodstone's Spectral Steed** (N) R: 10 yd; C: V,S,M; D: 1 hr/lvl; CT: 1 rd; AoE: Spcl; Save: None; TM37.
□ □ □ **Chain Lightning** (Ev) R: 40 yd+5 yd/lvl; C: V,S,M; D: Instant; CT: 5; AoE: Spcl; Save: ½; PH173.
□ □ □ **Claws of the Umber Hulk** (A) R: Touch; C: V,S,M; D: 1 tn/lvl; CT: 1 rd; AoE: 1 creature; Save: None; TM38.
□ □ □ **Conjure Animals** (C/S) R: 30 yd; C: V,S; D: 1 rd/lvl; CT: 6; AoE: Spcl; Save: None; PH174.
□ □ □ **Contingency** (Ev) R: 0; C: V,S,M; D: 1 d/lvl; CT: 1 tn; AoE: Caster; Save: None; PH174.
□ □ □ **Control Weather** (A, EA) R: 0; C: V,S,M; D: 4d6 hr; CT: 1 tn; AoE: 4d4 sq mi; Save: None; PH174.
□ □ □ **Death Fog** (A, Ev, EA) R: 30 yd; C: V,S,M; D: 1d4 rd+1 rd/lvl; CT: 6; AoE: Two 10′ cubes/lvl; Save: None; PH175.
□ □ □ **Death Spell** (N) R: 10 yd/lvl; C: V,S,M; D: Instant; CT: 6; AoE: One 30′ cube/lvl; Save: None; PH175.
□ □ □ **Demi-Shadow Magic** (I/P) R: 60 yd+10 yd/lvl; C: V,S; D: Spcl; CT: 6; AoE: Spcl; Save: Spcl; PH175.
□ □ □ **Dilation II** (A) R: 0; C: V; D: Spcl; CT: 5; AoE: Spcl; Save: None; TM38.
□ □ □ **Disintegrate** (A) R: 5 yd/lvl; C: V,S,M; D: Instant; CT: 6; AoE: Spcl; Save: Neg; PH175.
□ □ □ **Enchant an Item** (En, In) R: Touch; C: V,S,M; D: Spcl; CT: Spcl; AoE: 1 item; Save: Neg; PH175.
□ □ □ **Ensnarement** (C/S) R: 10 yd; C: V,S,M; D: Spcl; CT: 1 tn; AoE: Spcl; Save: Neg; PH176.
□ □ □ **Extension III** (A) R: 0; C: V; D: Spcl; CT: 6; AoE: Spcl; Save: None; PH177.
□ □ □ **Eyebite** (En/Ch, I/P) R: 20 yd; C: V,S; D: 1 rd/3 lvl; CT: 6; AoE: 1 creature; Save: Spcl; PH177.
□ □ □ **Forest's Fiery Constrictor** (C/S, EF) R: 10 yd/lvl; C: V,S,M; D: 1 rd/lvl; CT: 6; AoE: 1 source of fire; Save: Spcl; TM38.
□ □ □ **Geas** (En/Ch) R: 10 yd; C: V; D: Spcl; CT: 4; AoE: 1 creature; Save: None; PH177.
□ □ □ **Glassee** (A, EE) R: Touch; C: V,S,M; D: 1 rd/lvl; CT: 1 rd; AoE: Spcl; Save: None; PH177.
□ □ □ **Globe of Invulnerability** (Ab) R: 0; C: V,S,M; D: 1 rd/lvl; CT: 1 rd; AoE: 5′ radius; Save: None; PH177.
□ □ □ **Guards and Wards** (Ev, A, En/Ch) R: 0; C: V,S,M; D: 1 hr/lvl; CT: 3 tn; AoE: Spcl; Save: None; PH178.
□ □ □ **Invisible Stalker** (C/S) R: 10 yd; C: V,S,M; D: Spcl; CT: 1 rd; AoE: Spcl; Save: None; PH178.
□ □ □ **Legend Lore** (D) R: 0; C: V,S,M; D: Spcl; CT: Spcl; AoE: Spcl; Save: None; PH178.
□ □ □ **Lorloveim's Shadowy Transformation** (I) R: Touch; C: V,S; D: 1d4 rd+1 rd/lvl; CT: 6; AoE: Spcl; Save: Neg; TM38.
□ □ □ **Lower Water** (A, EW) R: 80 yd; C: V,S,M; D: 5 rd/lvl; CT: 1 tn; AoE: 10′ sq area/lvl; Save: None; PH178.
  □ □ □ ***Raise Water***
□ □ □ **Mass Suggestion** (En/Ch) R: 30 yd; C: V,M; D: 4 tn+4 tn/lvl; CT: 6; AoE: 1 creature/lvl; Save: Neg; PH179.
□ □ □ **Mirage Arcana** (I/P, A) R: 10 yd/lvl; C: V,S,(M optional); D: Spcl; CT: Spcl; AoE: 10′/lvl radius; Save: None; PH179.
□ □ □ **Mislead** (I/P) R: 10 yd; C: S; D: 1 rd/lvl; CT: 1 tn; AoE: Spcl; Save: None; PH179.
□ □ □ **Monster Summoning IV** (C/S) R: 60 yd; C: V,S,M; D: 5 rd+1 rd/lvl; CT: 6; AoE: Spcl; Save: None; PH179.
□ □ □ **Mordenkainen's Lucubration** (A) R: 0; C: V,S; D: Instant; CT: 1; AoE: Caster; Save: None; PH179.
□ □ □ **Move Earth** (A, EE) R: 10 yd/lvl; C: V,S,M; D: Perm; CT: Spcl; AoE: Spcl; Save: None; PH179.
□ □ □ **Otiluke's Freezing Sphere** (A, Ev, EW) R: Spcl; C: V,S,M; D: Spcl; CT: 6; AoE: Spcl; Save: Spcl; PH180.
□ □ □ **Part Water** (A, EW) R: 10 yd/lvl; C: V,S,M; D: 5 rd/lvl; CT: 1 tn; AoE: Spcl; Save: None; PH180.
□ □ □ **Permanent Illusion** (I/P) R: 10 yd/lvl; C: V,S,M; D: Perm; CT: 6; AoE: 20′ cube+10′ cube/lvl; Save: Spcl; PH180.
□ □ □ **Programmed Illusion** (I/P) R: 10 yd/lvl; C: V,S,M; D: Spcl; CT: 6; AoE: 20′ cube+10′ cube/lvl; Save: Spcl; PH180.
□ □ □ **Project Image** (A, I/P) R: 10 yd/lvl; C: V,S,M; D: 1 rd/lvl; CT: 6; AoE: Spcl; Save: None; PH180.
□ □ □ **Reincarnation** (N) R: Touch; C: V,S,M; D: Perm; CT: 1 tn; AoE: Person touched; Save: None; PH181.
□ □ □ **Repulsion** (Ab) R: 10 yd/lvl; C: V,S,M; D: 1 rd/2 lvl; CT: 6; AoE: Creatures in a 10′-wide path; Save: None; PH181.
□ □ □ **Shades** (I/P) R: 30 yd; C: V,S; D: 1 rd/lvl; CT: 6; AoE: 20′ cube; Save: Spcl; PH181.
□ □ □ **Stone to Flesh** (A, EE) R: 10 yd/lvl; C: V,S,M; D: Perm; CT: 6; AoE: 1 creature; Save: Spcl; PH181.
  □ □ □ ***Flesh to Stone***
□ □ □ **Tenser's Transformation** (A, Ev) R: 0; C: V,S,M; D: 1 rd/lvl; CT: 6; AoE: Caster; Save: None; PH181.
□ □ □ **Transmute Water to Dust** (A, EE, EW) R: 60 yd; C: V,S,M; D: Perm; CT: 5; AoE: One 10′ cube/lvl; Save: None (spcl); PH182.
  □ □ □ ***Transmute Dust to Water***
□ □ □ **True Seeing** (D) R: Touch; C: V,S,M; D: 1 rd/lvl; CT: 1 rd; AoE: 60′ light range; Save: None; PH182.
□ □ □ **Veil** (I/P) R: 10 yd/lvl; C: V,S; D: 1 tn/lvl; CT: 6; AoE: 20′ cube/lvl; Save: None; PH182.